Navigating the Storm:

A Guide for Parents on Supporting Teenagers with Depression

By Diane Carla

Table of contents

Chapter 1 :The In depth truth about depression

Chapter 2 :Understanding the adolescent mind

Chapter 3: Your role as a parent

Chapter 4: Strategies to help your teenager navigate the emotional rollercoaster

Chapter 5: Bridging the gap in your relationship with your teenager

Chapter 6: Raising productive and healthy young adults

Chapter 1 :The In depth truth about depression

Depression is a common and serious mental health condition that can cause a wide range of emotional and physical symptoms. It can affect people of all ages and is often accompanied by feelings of sadness, hopelessness, and a lack of interest in activities that were once enjoyable. Depression can also cause physical symptoms such as changes in appetite, sleep patterns, and energy levels.

There is no single cause of depression. It is likely caused by a combination of genetic, environmental, and psychological factors. Some people may be more vulnerable to developing depression due to their genes, while others may develop the condition as a result of life experiences such as trauma, abuse, or loss.

Depression is not just feeling sad or down. It is a serious mental illness that can cause a variety of physical and emotional symptoms, including changes in sleep patterns, loss of appetite, difficulty concentrating, feelings of worthlessness or hopelessness, and thoughts of suicide.

Depression can be caused by a variety of factors, including genetics, life events, and medical conditions. It is not always clear why someone develops depression, and it is often a combination of factors.

Depression is not a sign of weakness or a character flaw. It is a medical condition that requires treatment, just like any other illness.

There are effective treatments for depression, including medications, talk therapy, and other forms of psychological treatment. It is important to seek help from a qualified professional if you think you may be experiencing depression.

Depression is common. It is estimated that around 10% of adults in the US experience depression at some point in their lives. However, it is also treatable, and many people are able to recover with the right help and support.

Depression is a serious medical condition that can cause significant impairment in daily functioning and can even lead to thoughts of suicide.

There are several types of depression, including:

Major depressive disorder: This is the most severe form of depression, characterized by a combination of symptoms that interfere with daily life and activities.

Persistent depressive disorder (formerly known as dysthymia): This is a long-term form of depression that lasts for at least two years.

Bipolar disorder: This is a condition that involves periods of depression and periods of elevated mood (mania).

Seasonal affective disorder (SAD): This form of depression is characterized by symptoms that occur during the winter months when there is less natural sunlight.

Depression is a treatable condition, and there are a number of effective treatments available. These may include medication, such as antidepressants, and talk therapy, such as cognitive behavioral therapy (CBT) or interpersonal therapy (IPT). Treatment is often most effective when it combines both medication and therapy.

It is important to seek help if you or someone you know is experiencing symptoms of depression. Depression can be severe and can lead to serious problems if left untreated. With the right treatment, however, most people with depression can improve and lead fulfilling, productive lives.

Chapter 2 :Understanding the adolescent mind

Adolescence is a period of significant psychological, social, and biological development that occurs during the transition from childhood to adulthood. During this time, the adolescent mind undergoes significant changes that can affect a person's cognitive, emotional, and social functioning.

One key aspect of the adolescent mind is its increased capacity for abstract thinking and problem-solving. Adolescents are able to think more critically and logically, and are better able to consider multiple viewpoints and perspectives. This allows them to make more complex decisions and to better understand and solve problems in their environment.

At the same time, the adolescent mind is also characterized by increased emotional intensity and sensitivity. Adolescents may experience a wider range of emotions and may have more difficulty regulating their emotions, which can lead to mood swings and erratic behavior. They may also be more sensitive to social and peer pressure, and may be more influenced by the opinions and behaviors of their peers.

Adolescents also tend to be more self-conscious and concerned about their appearance and reputation, and may be more concerned about their social status and identity. They may also be more focused on achieving independence and autonomy, and may be more resistant to authority and rules.

Overall, the adolescent mind is complex and multifaceted, and is characterized by significant changes in cognitive, emotional, and social functioning as the individual transitions from childhood to adulthood.

Adolescents today face a wide range of challenges and problems, many of which are similar to those faced by adolescents in the past. Some common problems that adolescents may face include:

Academic stress: Many adolescents struggle with academic pressure and may feel overwhelmed by the demands of schoolwork and exams.

Peer pressure: Adolescents may feel pressure to conform to the expectations and behaviors of their peers, which can lead to risky or unhealthy behaviors.

Identity development: Adolescents may struggle with developing a sense of identity and may feel uncertain about their goals and values.

Mental health issues: Adolescents may experience mental health issues such as anxiety, depression, or eating disorders, which can significantly impact their well-being.

Substance abuse: Some adolescents may experiment with drugs or alcohol, which can lead to addiction and other serious problems.

Social media and technology: The proliferation of social media and technology can create new challenges for adolescents, such as cyberbullying and the pressure to present a certain image online.

Family conflict: Adolescents may experience conflict with their parents or other family members as they seek more independence and autonomy.

Physical health issues: Adolescents may face physical health issues such as obesity, eating disorders, or sexually transmitted infections.

It's important to note that these problems are not necessarily unique to adolescents, and many individuals of all ages may face similar challenges. However, the developmental changes that occur during adolescence can make these problems particularly difficult for adolescents to navigate.

Chapter 3: Your role as a parent

The roles of a parent are diverse and can vary greatly depending on the specific needs and circumstances of a family. However, some common roles that parents may play include:

Nurturer and caregiver: Parents provide physical care and support to their children, including feeding, bathing, dressing, and providing a safe and comfortable living environment.

Teacher and mentor: Parents are responsible for helping their children learn and grow, both academically and socially. This includes teaching them important life skills, values, and behaviors.

Role model: Parents serve as role models for their children, and the way they behave and interact with others can have a significant impact on their children's development.

Protector: Parents are responsible for keeping their children safe from harm and ensuring their well-being. This includes protecting them from physical danger and providing a supportive and nurturing environment.

Discipline provider: Parents are responsible for setting limits and boundaries for their children and helping them learn to make good choices. This may involve setting rules and consequences for behavior.

Advocate: Parents are often the primary advocates for their children, speaking up for them and advocating for their needs and best interests.

Support system: Parents should be there for their children, providing emotional support and guidance as they navigate life's challenges.

Overall, the roles of a parent are multifaceted and can vary greatly depending on the specific needs of a child and family. The most important thing is for parents to be loving, supportive, and involved in their children's lives.

Being a parent means taking on the responsibility of raising and caring for a child. This involves providing for their physical needs, such as food, clothing, and shelter, as well as their emotional and social needs, such as love, support, and guidance.

As a parent, you play a crucial role in shaping your child's development and helping them grow into a responsible and independent adult. This requires patience, understanding, and a willingness to listen and communicate with your child.

Being a parent also involves setting boundaries and teaching your child right from wrong, as well as helping them develop self-discipline and coping skills. It means being there for your child through the ups and downs of life, offering support and encouragement as they learn and grow.

In short, being a parent is a challenging, but rewarding, role that involves caring for and nurturing the next generation. It requires a strong commitment and a willingness to put your child's needs above your own.

There are many expectations that society and culture place on parents, and these can vary greatly depending on the specific context and community in which they live. In general, however, parents are expected to provide for the basic needs of their children, including food, shelter, clothing, and medical care. They are also expected to protect their children from harm and to provide a safe and nurturing environment for them to grow and develop.

In addition to meeting these basic needs, parents are also expected to support their children's physical, emotional, and intellectual development. This may include encouraging and helping their children to learn new things, teaching them important life skills, and providing guidance and support as they navigate the challenges and transitions of growing up.

Parents are also often expected to set a good example for their children, by demonstrating positive behaviors and values and by teaching their children how to be responsible, respectful, and compassionate members of society. Finally, parents are expected to maintain open and honest communication with their children and to foster strong, positive relationships with them.

Chapter 4: Strategies to help your teenager navigate the emotional rollercoaster

Here are some strategies that parents can use to help their teenagers navigate the emotional rollercoaster of adolescence:

Encourage open communication: Encourage your teenager to talk about their feelings and listen actively without judgment. This can help them feel heard and understood, which can be very important during the tumultuous teenage years.

Offer support and guidance: Let your teenager know that you are there to support and guide them through any challenges they may face.

Offer advice when asked for it, but also be open to hearing their own ideas and perspectives.

Help them develop coping skills: Help your teenager develop coping skills such as problem-solving, stress management, and emotion regulation. These skills will be valuable throughout their life and can help them navigate the challenges of adolescence.

Encourage healthy habits: Encourage your teenager to engage in healthy habits such as exercise, getting enough sleep, and eating a balanced diet. These habits can help improve their overall well-being and help them cope with the challenges of adolescence.

Set boundaries: Establish clear boundaries and expectations for your teenager's behavior. This can help them feel more secure and help them understand what is acceptable and what is not.

Be a role model: Be a positive role model for your teenager. Show them how to cope with challenges and emotions in a healthy way.

Seek outside help: If you feel like you are unable to support your teenager or if you are concerned about their mental health, don't hesitate to seek outside help from a mental health professional.

Model emotional intelligence: As a parent, it's important to model healthy ways of expressing and managing emotions. This can involve acknowledging and labeling your own emotions, and demonstrating healthy coping mechanisms when you're feeling upset.

Encourage self-reflection: Help your teenager develop self-awareness by encouraging them to reflect on their emotions and the situations that lead to them. This can help them better understand their emotional triggers and how to manage them.

Encourage mindfulness: Mindfulness practices, such as meditation and deep breathing, can help teenagers become more attuned to their emotions and the present moment. Encourage your teenager to try mindfulness exercises and discuss their experiences with them.

Chapter 5: Bridging the gap in your relationship with your teenager

Adolescence can be a challenging time for both parents and kids. During this period, it is normal for kids to seek more independence and for parents to feel a sense of loss as their children become more independent. However, it is important for parents to continue to be a supportive and caring presence in their children's lives. Here are a few tips for how parents can stay connected with their kids during adolescence:

Make time for one-on-one activities: Adolescents often appreciate having quality time with their parents, whether it's going for a hike, cooking a meal together, or simply having a heart-to-heart conversation.

Be there for your child: It is important for parents to be available and responsive to their children's needs and to show that they care. This can involve actively listening to their concerns, offering guidance and support, and being there for them when they need someone to talk to.

Communicate openly and honestly: Adolescents often have a lot of questions and may be struggling with complex emotions and issues. It is important for parents to be open and honest with their children, and to provide accurate and age-appropriate information.

Chapter 6: Raising productive and healthy young adults

There are many keys to successful parenting, and what works for one family may not work for another. However, there are some general principles that can help you raise happy, healthy, and well-adjusted children:

Love and support: Show your children that you love them unconditionally and provide them with the emotional and physical support they need to grow and develop.

Communication: Encourage open and honest communication with your children, listen to them, and be available to talk to them when they need it.

Consistency: Establish clear rules and expectations, and be consistent in enforcing them. This helps children feel secure and understand what is expected of them.

Flexibility: Be open to trying new approaches and adapting your parenting style to your child's changing needs.

Patience: Parenting can be challenging at times, so it's important to be patient with your children and yourself.

Self-care: Make sure to take care of yourself emotionally and physically, as this will help you be a better parent.

Seek support: Don't be afraid to ask for help or advice from trusted friends, family, or professionals when you need it.

Remember, every family is different, and what works for one family may not work for another.

It's important to find what works best for you and your children.